Breakthroughs
IN SCIENCE AND TECHNOLOGY

Who Discovered
Natural Selection?

Who Discovered
Natural Selection?

Anna Claybourne

ARCTURUS

This edition first published in 2010 by Arcturus Publishing
Distributed by Black Rabbit Books
P.O. Box 3263
Mankato, Minnesota 56002

Printed in China

Planned and produced by Discovery Books Ltd.
www.discoverybooks.net
Managing editor: Laura Durman
Editors: Amy Bauman and Penny Worms
Designer: Ian Winton
Illustrator: Stefan Chabluk

Library of Congress Cataloging-in-Publication Data

Claybourne, Anna.
  Who discovered natural selection? / Anna Claybourne.
    p. cm. – (Breakthroughs in science and technology)
  Includes index.
  Summary: "Looking at some of the major inventions and discoveries shaping our world today, Breakthroughs in Science profiles the research leading up to the discovery (not just profiles of the one or two key "players"). Each book describes the "famous" moment and then examines the continued evolution illustrating its impact today and for the future"– Provided by publisher.
  ISBN 978-1-84837-682-3 (lib. bdg.)
 1. Natural selection–Juvenile literature. 2. Darwin, Charles, 1809-1882–Juvenile literature. 3. Genes–Juvenile literature. 4. Discoveries in science–Juvenile literature. I. Title.
  QH375.C53 2011
  576.8'2–dc22

                        2010011020

Picture credits
Corbis: 10 (Stefano Bianchetti), 14 (Visuals Unlimited), 15, 21 top (Hulton-Deutsch Collection), 24 (William Perlman/Star Ledger), 31 (EPA/Andy Rain), 37 (Bettmann), 40 (CDC/C. S. Goldsmith and A. Balish).
FLPA: 30 top (Chris Mattison).
Getty Images: 19 (Joseph Wright of Derby), 21 bottom (George Richmond).
istockphoto.com: 17 right (John Pitcher), 18 (Daniel Wrench), 23 (Richard Waghorn), 25 (stockcam), 33 (Hulton Archive), 43 (Peter Malsbury).
National Science Foundation: 16 (Nicolle Rager Fuller).
Shutterstock Images: cover (Michael Klenetsky), title page and 12 (Dennis Donohue), 7 (Seleznev Oleg), 9 (markrhiggins), 13 (Rich Koele), 17 left (Utekhina Anna), 26 (NREY), 28 (worldswildlifewonders), 29 (Alex Edmonds), 35 (B. G. Smith), 36 (Mushakesa), 38 (Monkey Business Images), 41 (Christopher Halloran).
Science Photo Library: 6 (Christian Darkin), 11, 22, 32 (Bill Sanderson), 39 (A. Barrington Brown), 42 (Hazel Appleton, Centre for Infections/Health Protection Agency).
Wikimedia Commons: 8, 20 bottom (Conrad Martens), 30 bottom, 34.

Every attempt has been made to clear copyright. Should there be any inadvertent omission, please apply to the publisher for rectification.

SL001448US   Supplier 03, Date 0510

Contents

What is natural selection?

An important question

Why do the animals, plants, and people on our planet look and act the way they do? And why are there so many different types, or **species**, of living things? These are among the most important questions in science—especially **biology**, the science of life. For most scientists, the answer is **natural selection**.

Discovering the world

The **theory** of natural selection developed in the 1800s. This was a time when scientists and explorers were finding out more and more about the natural world, and its plants, animals, and other creatures such as fungi and **bacteria**.

From **fossils**, they also learned about the creatures that lived on the earth a long time ago. They wondered why some of these, such as dinosaurs, were so different from modern life-forms. Had living things been changing, or evolving, all this time? And if they had, how?

Finding an answer

Several scientists came up with interesting ideas, but the most famous of them all was Charles Darwin, and the

This artwork shows the giant Megalodon shark, the biggest fish ever. The shark lived between 25 and 1.6 million years ago, and fossils show it was 66 feet (20 m) long. A modern white shark (also shown) measures around 20 feet (6 m).

The camel has evolved to become adapted to desert life and can survive for many days without food or water. It can also withstand the extreme temperatures in the desert, and its wide feet help it walk on soft sand.

theory he named "natural selection." Today Darwin's work is seen as one of the most important scientific discoveries ever made. However, not everyone agrees with everything Darwin said, and his theory still causes arguments.

> *"I have called this principle, by which each slight variation, if useful, is preserved, by the term of Natural Selection."*
> Charles Darwin, from *On the Origin of Species*, published 1859.

How natural selection works

So, what is this theory? It will be explained again later, but here is a simple version.

In any species, some individuals will be better at surviving than others. For example, some rabbits can run faster than others and are better at escaping from **predators**. Those that survive longest will be more likely to have plenty of young. They pass on their qualities, such as big, strong back legs, to their young.

In this way, nature "selects" the most useful qualities in a species. Over a long time, as this happens over and over again, the species changes, or evolves.

What is evolution?

Evolution is a word that means gradual change in a series of stages. By the 1800s, most scientists agreed that living things must have evolved over time. Natural selection is not the same thing as evolution, but it is a way of explaining how evolution happens.

Early ideas

Ancient thinkers and evolution

Several ancient thinkers wondered why there were so many living things, and why, judging by the fossils they found, life seemed to be so different from long ago. Some of their ideas came remarkably close to what we now believe is the truth.

Out of the mud

Anaximander, an ancient Greek who lived more than 2,500 years ago, decided that living things had developed from sea mud. He also said that humans didn't exist at first but developed from fish. Like many Greeks, Anaximander did not have much evidence for his ideas. However, this was one of the first attempts to explain evolution.

Dying out

Another great Greek, Empedocles, and the later Roman writer Lucretius, suggested that some creatures that had once been alive were poor at surviving, or not useful, and had died out. This early theory is similar to Darwin's ideas on natural selection.

The changing earth

Some early scientists saw that the earth had changed over time. Anaximander's student, Xenophanes, found seashell fossils in rocks on dry land, and realized

Empedocles

Date of birth: c. 495 B.C.

Place of birth: Probably Sicily

Greatest achievements: Although most of his work has long since been lost, traditionally, he was famous for two long poems. The first, "On Nature," was about how all living things were created from four "elements"—earth, air, fire, and water. "Purifications," the second poem, was concerned with religion.

Interesting fact: Scholars today think the two poems may actually have been one long one.

Date of death: c. 435 B.C.

THAT'S A FACT!

Many ancient stories about how the earth and all living things came into being tell of a time when there was nothing but water. Today, many scientists believe that all life first evolved in water.

that this land had once been covered by sea. Around the year A.D. 1,000 Chinese scientist Shen Kuo and Persian thinker Ibn Sina both came up with the idea that rocks moving and changing over time were responsible for the shape of the land on earth.

Fossils, like these of fish, convinced scientists in the ancient world that the earth must have changed over time. They realized that rocks now found on land must have once been under the sea.

These ideas later became very important to the theory of natural selection, as they showed that the world was very old and there had been plenty of time for living things to evolve.

Breakthrough

These earliest ideas about evolution challenged long-held traditional beliefs about how life on earth was created. They may not have been exactly right, but they paved the way for later scientists.

Evidence of the past

Fossils are one of the biggest clues that life today is not the same as it once was. While some early thinkers, such as Xenophanes, used fossils as evidence for scientific ideas, they also led to many myths and stories. Dragons, for example, which appear in the **folklore** of many different cultures, may have been invented as an explanation for dinosaur fossils.

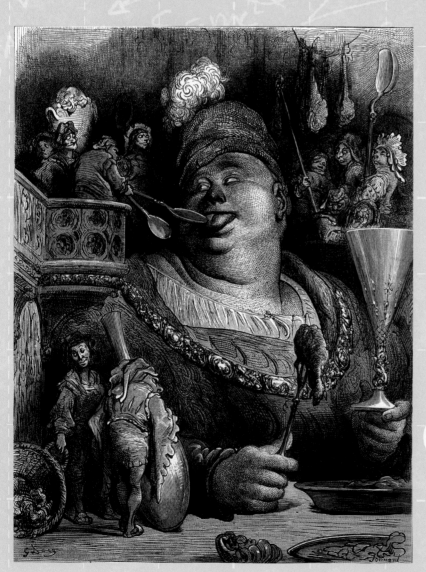

Fossil-hunting fever

From the 1600s, scientists began to take fossils seriously as a part of scientific study. Fossil hunters such as William Buckland, Gideon Mantell, and Mary Anning became famous for their discoveries. There was much debate about what these ancient remains were, and why the creatures they came from were no longer around.

The giant's thighbone

In 1676, someone sent a fossil bone found near Oxford,

This picture by Gustave Doré illustrates a story of human-like giants. Giants figure in the folklore of many countries around the world. The myths may have developed as a way to explain the discovery of large fossils.

Mary Anning

Date of birth: May 21, 1799

Place of birth: Lyme Regis, England

Greatest achievement: Anning's discovery of important ichthyosaur and plesiosaur fossils.

Interesting fact: After her father died in 1810, Mary Anning sold her fossil finds to scientists in order to support her family. She became so respected that she was given honorary membership in the Geological Society of London—which women were not normally allowed to join.

Date of death: March 9, 1847

> *"If then they are neither the Bones of Horses, Oxen, nor Elephants, as I am strongly persuaded they are not . . . It remains, that (notwithstanding their extravagant Magnitude) they must have been the bones of Men or Women."*

Robert Plot in his book *The Natural History of Oxfordshire* (published 1705), writing about where the giant thigh bones could have come from.

England, to a scientist named Robert Plot to study. Until then, Plot thought fossils were nothing to do with ancient creatures, but were just chance formations in rock. But when he saw the new fossil, he changed his mind. He realized it looked exactly like the lower end of a human **femur**, or thighbone—but much too big.

At first, he thought it might be from an elephant. Then he changed his mind and decided it had belonged to a giant human. We now know that it came from a type of dinosaur called Megalosaurus.

Breakthrough

Robert Plot's discoveries and descriptions of fossils opened up a whole new area of science: the study of prehistoric life. This was to become known as paleontology.

Evolution: the great debate

The evidence grows

So, had life changed over time, or not? As the 1700s and 1800s went on, there seemed to be very clear evidence from fossils that it had. All kinds of creatures were being discovered that no one had ever seen alive or that were much bigger than their present-day descendants. Life, it seemed, must have been evolving for many years.

Religious worries

However, many people did not like the idea of evolution at all, because it cast doubt on their religious beliefs. Many Christians held the traditional belief that a **divine** being created all life-forms just as they are now. If evolution was true, could religious teaching be wrong?

The debate

As scientists came up with more ideas and evidence, a great debate began about whether evolution had really happened at all. Among the important points in this debate were the following:

1778: French **naturalist** Georges-Louis Leclerc (1707–88) claimed that evolution was true, and in fact all life had evolved from a single, first life-form.

Giraffes' long necks enable them to reach the leaves of the trees from which they feed. Scientist Jean-Baptiste Lamarck believed that their ancestors had stretched their necks by reaching upward and then passed this feature on to their young.

1809: Another Frenchman, Jean-Baptiste Lamarck (1744–1829), developed a theory of evolution that said animals changed slowly within their lifetimes and then passed on these changes to their young.

1817: The great fossil expert Georges Cuvier (1769–1832) said the fossils he had studied were very old and the creatures were now **extinct**. He also showed how some prehistoric extinct creatures looked similar to, but not the same as, modern animals. These included, for example, woolly mammoths resembling modern elephants. Although many scientists were aware of this, it was still a controversial idea.

A fossil skull of a mammoth. The paleontologist Georges Cuvier noted how woolly mammoths, which died out around 5,000 years ago, resembled modern elephants.

"Would it not . . . be glorious for man to burst the limits of time, and, by a few observations, to ascertain the history of this world, and the series of events which preceded the birth of the human race?"
Georges Cuvier in *Researches on Fossil Bones* **(published 1812).**

Some Christian leaders argued against these scientists, and in some cases forced them to retract (take back) what they had said. The Christian leaders claimed that some animals were no longer with us because of Noah's flood, which also explained why sea fossils were found on dry land. However, that didn't explain why so many sea creatures had died out, too. How could the flood account for fossils of ancient sharks and other sea creatures, which should have survived it?

Breakthrough

Georges Cuvier's studies revealed a huge amount about what prehistoric life had actually been like, and how different it was from today. The prehistoric animals he discovered included woolly mammoths and giant sloths.

How old is the earth?

Another argument took place in the 1700s and 1800s about the age of the earth. If the theory of evolution were true, many scientists thought the earth must be very old indeed, to allow time for all the changes to happen. Georges-Louis Leclerc estimated the earth to be at least 10 million years old.

Evidence in rocks

By the end of the 1700s, **geologists** (scientists who study the earth) had begun finding evidence that showed how the earth itself must have changed over a very long time.

THAT'S A FACT!

In the 1650s, an Irish archbishop named James Ussher worked out the age of the earth by counting up all the ages of the characters in the Bible. He came to the conclusion that God had created the world in exactly 4004 B.C. Not all Christians believed him— but there were some who did.

The different layers of rock in this cliff formed from mud and sand one on top of another over millions of years. Some of these layers contain fossils of creatures that got trapped in the mud.

By studying rock formations, Scottish geologist James Hutton saw that some rocks had formed in layers and then lifted, tilted, and folded. He noted that others were formed from melted rock from volcanoes that had cooled.

24

A. Int. 1787

William Smith

In the late 1700s, William Smith worked out how the age of fossils revealed the age of the layers of rock they were found in, and vice versa. This began the "fossil record" system that helps us figure out the age of rocks and fossils.

Hutton also realized that, as old rocks were worn away by wind and rain, layers of mud formed new rock on the seabed. Hutton thought these processes happened again and again, in a huge cycle, and had happened so many times that the earth must be many millions of years old. This theory is known as **uniformitarianism**.

Charles Lyell

Hutton's ideas were not widely accepted or understood when he first published them in the 1780s. But 50 years later, another geologist from Scotland, Charles Lyell, backed them up and made them better known. Lyell was to become a friend of Charles Darwin (see pages 18–35), who was strongly influenced by his work.

Breakthrough

Hutton's theory of uniformitarianism meant the earth's age must be much greater than anyone had previously thought.

Making living things change

In the argument about evolution, another factor played a big part. Although there was a debate about evolution in the natural world, and whether it even existed, it was known that people could make animal and plant species change over time.

Selecting the best

For thousands of years, farmers and gardeners had been practicing **selective breeding**. Quite simply, they selected the individual plants and animals they liked best and used them to breed from. For example, a pig farmer would breed piglets from the plumpest, healthiest pigs, while an apple grower would select the apple tree with the juiciest, sweetest apples, and use its seeds to grow new trees.

Even in ancient times, people knew from experience that living things passed on their qualities to their offspring. So selective breeding helped farmers weed

Cultivated maize of the kind shown on the right was developed from a wild form, called teosinte (left), more than 6,000 years ago. Teosinte had many seed heads with small seeds in hard cases. Careful breeding by farmers changed it to the modern form, which has no branches. It has fewer, bigger seed heads, with large, soft seeds.

From wolves to dogs

Think of all the different dog breeds you've ever seen, from tiny Chihuahuas to huge Labradors. They were all developed from a single wild species, a type of wolf. It was first domesticated around 12,000 years ago, as an animal that could help with hunting.

Over many years, people used selective breeding to develop different breeds with qualities suitable for various purposes, such as guarding homes or animals, racing, fighting, hunting, and so on.

out less useful varieties and grow more of the most useful ones. Over time, many types of crops and farm animals changed beyond recognition. For example, crops like wheat, carrots, and apples started out as wild plants with very small, edible parts. Centuries of selective breeding made them change shape and size, creating the modern fruits and vegetables we know today.

Pioneer on the farm

Farm animals were domesticated later than dogs. It was not until the 1700s that farmers began to think seriously about producing specialist breeds of animals such as sheep and cattle—breeds that produced especially good meat, for example, or (in the case of sheep) better wool. One pioneer in this was the English farmer Robert Bakewell, who also started the practice of hiring out male animals to help other farmers improve their stock.

Breakthrough

The process of humans deliberately selecting animals to breed from was part of a huge change in human life, when people stopped relying on hunting and gathering and took up farming instead. Farmers such as Robert Bakewell were among the first to create really specialized breeds of farm animals.

Pulling the ideas together

By the beginning of the 1800s, many scientists had begun to understand that the earth and the life it supported had changed over long periods of time. A number of ideas about how evolution might have taken place had been suggested. However, it would take the right person to put it all together and make sense of it. That person was Charles Darwin.

A hopeless case?

Charles Darwin was born into a wealthy English family in 1809. His parents hoped he would be a doctor like his father, Robert Darwin. But when young Charles was growing up, Robert lost hope in him. Studying and school bored Charles, and he seemed lazy and useless. He went on to the University of Edinburgh, Scotland, to study medicine, and when that failed, was sent to Cambridge, England, to study to be a clergyman—but he was still unhappy.

> "... no pursuit at Cambridge ... gave me so much pleasure as collecting beetles. ... No poet ever felt more delighted at seeing his first poem published than I did at seeing, in Stephens' Illustrations of British Insects, the magic words, 'captured by C. Darwin, Esq.'"
>
> Charles Darwin, from his autobiography, published in 1887.

A statue of Charles Darwin, outside the building in Shrewsbury, in England, where he went to school. Darwin showed little promise as a schoolboy—but eventually became one of the most important scientists ever.

Erasmus Darwin

Darwin was not the first person in his family to take an interest in the natural world. His grandfather, Erasmus Darwin, a doctor and biologist, had published his own ideas on evolution in the late 1700s. In a theory similar to Leclerc's, he wrote: "Would it be too bold to imagine that all warm-blooded animals have arisen from one living filament, which the great First Cause endued with animality?" In other words, he suggested that many living things had evolved from a single ancestor.

taxidermist, who lived just across the street from his lodgings. At Cambridge, he spent a lot of time shooting birds in the countryside (a common pastime in those days) and collecting beetles. He also made friends with John Henslow, a plant scientist, whose botany lectures Darwin attended. It was clear that what Darwin loved most was to study and discuss his true passion—the natural world.

Natural friends

Darwin's real interest was in nature and the countryside. As a boy, he had spent many vacations hiking in North Wales and had always been a keen collector of shells, minerals, and insects. At Edinburgh, he made friends with a naturalist, Robert Grant, who was an expert on sea creatures, and John Edmonstone, a

The chance of a lifetime

Then in 1831, when Darwin was just 22, his friend John Henslow recommended him for the post of ship's naturalist on the *Beagle*, a **survey ship** sailing the world to **chart** coastlines. Darwin's father was not eager for him to put off his career even longer. But one of Darwin's uncles persuaded Robert to let his son join the voyage.

The voyage of the Beagle

Round the world

HMS *Beagle*, captained by Robert Fitzroy, and with the young Charles Darwin on board, set off from Plymouth, England, on December 27, 1831. It eventually went all the way around the world, sailing for almost five years before returning home.

Darwin and Fitzroy

Fitzroy wanted Darwin on board for several reasons—to collect nature and wildlife samples, to chart the rocks and **landforms** of the places they visited, and to be a traveling companion and dining partner. Darwin and Fitzroy did become good friends, though they often disagreed and had some violent arguments. Sadly, when Darwin's theory of natural selection was eventually published, Fitzroy was horrified by it, and their friendship was over.

Heading west

Like many voyages of exploration before it, the *Beagle's* journey began by crossing the Atlantic to the Americas. On the way, the ship stopped at several islands, including the Canaries and the Cape Verde Islands. Darwin began work as soon as he could, studying seabirds and tropical plants.

Arctic Ocean

North America

Europe

Asia

Atlantic Ocean

Pacific Ocean

Africa

Pacific Ocean

South America

Indian Ocean

GALAPAGOS ISLANDS

Australia

2000 miles

2000 kilometers

Southern Ocean

Antarctica

The map above shows the route of the *Beagle's* five-year voyage, during which Darwin started to form his ideas about evolution. The painting (right) shows the *Beagle* at the tip of South America—a region called Tierra del Fuego.

Robert Fitzroy

Date of birth: July 5, 1805

Place of birth: Ampton, England

Greatest achievement: Though most famous for being captain on board the *Beagle*, Fitzroy also became governor of New Zealand and was an important expert on weather.

Interesting fact: Fitzroy was one of the first to find reliable ways of predicting the weather, and he invented the term "weather forecasting."

Date of death: April 30, 1865

THAT'S A FACT!

When Fitzroy first met Darwin (below), he didn't like him, because he thought the stubby shape of his nose revealed a weak personality. This was a common belief at the time. However, Fitzroy later changed his mind.

Even before the ship landed on any shore, Darwin had strung a net behind it so that he could collect and study **plankton** and other sea creatures. On land, he studied rock **strata** (layers).

The *Beagle* sailed around the world, visiting many parts of South America including the Brazilian rain forest, the Falkland Islands, Patagonia, and the Galapagos Islands. The voyage continued to Australia, the Cocos Islands, and southern Africa. Darwin was able to sketch, collect, and compare natural phenomena from a wide range of **habitats** and continents.

Breakthrough

Almost from the start, Charles Darwin's experiences on the voyage of the *Beagle* planted important ideas in his mind. He began to see that different life-forms were somehow related and seemed to have developed over time.

Darwin's discoveries

A record of the voyage

During the voyage of the *Beagle*, Darwin made many fascinating, puzzling, and important discoveries. He kept records of everything he could, filling notebooks with notes and sketches and collecting thousands of samples to be sent back to Britain.

A world of wondrous sights

Darwin saw many amazing sights during the voyage. Here are just a few of them:

• On St. Jago, in the Cape Verde Islands, he saw a layer of ancient sea fossils high up in a cliff face. Like his friend, Charles Lyell, he thought this meant the land must have risen over time.

• In Argentina, he studied fossils of prehistoric animals much bigger than

modern ones, such as giant sloths. Had these species changed over time, he wondered? Why would they have changed?

• The Falkland Islands reminded Darwin of Wales, and the fossils and wildlife he found there were like those in Wales, too. He wondered whether a landscape could affect the kinds of animals that lived in it.

Darwin himself made these drawings of the heads and beaks of some of the different finches he saw on various Galapagos Islands. Darwin realized that the birds all had a common ancestor, but the beaks were adapted to suit the kinds of food available on the different islands.

The Galapagos Islands are famous for their giant tortoises. There are several kinds— each with different-shaped shells, adapted to the varied habitats on different islands.

• In the Galapagos Islands, Darwin learned that finches (a type of small bird) were slightly different on each island. Why was this?

• In Australia, Darwin noted many unique, wild species, such as platypuses and kangaroos. He wondered why they were so unlike animals in the rest of the world.

Darwin made notes on the different peoples he met. He concluded that people were different from each other only because of their different cultures. Underneath that, all humans were mostly the same and were just a type of animal, along with many other living things.

Breakthrough

Darwin's famous discovery of similar-looking but distinct species of finches on the different Galapagos Islands was to be of huge importance. It would become a key part of the development of his groundbreaking natural selection theory.

The end of the voyage

The *Beagle* finally returned to England on October 2, 1836, docking at Falmouth in Cornwall.

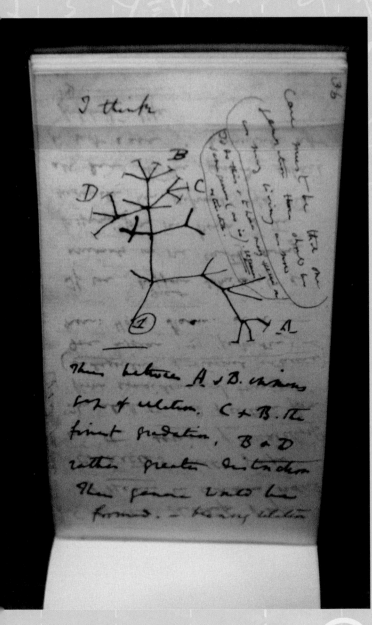

This sketch, showing the "tree of life," appears in one of Charles Darwin's journals. In it, he shows how all life-forms can be seen as "branches" springing from a single stem.

Darwin was still just 27 but, during his five-year journey on the *Beagle*, he had already become well-known among scientists because of all the letters, sketches, and nature samples he had sent home. His friends at Britain's great universities and museums were already discussing what his findings could mean.

Ideas in the making

Upon his return, Darwin kept fairly quiet about his ideas. He believed living things had changed over time and that today's species had developed and branched off from older species. But he had not yet determined what made this happen.

It became his life's work to find out. He was beginning to develop a theory about evolution—but he knew this was very controversial, and he needed clear evidence and a strong argument.

THAT'S A FACT!

After the *Beagle* docked, Charles Darwin immediately set off to his family home in Shropshire. He arrived late at night, sneaked into the house, and went to bed. Then he surprised his family by strolling casually into the room the next morning as they were having breakfast.

Luckily for Darwin, his father saw that he really did have a focus in life now and gave him an allowance. He no longer demanded that his son become a doctor or a clergyman. So Charles settled down. He began working through all his notes and sketches and exchanging letters with friends whom he could trust as he worked out his theories.

Darwin's first book

In 1839—the year of his marriage—Darwin published a book of his travel

Darwin bought Down House, Kent (shown here) in 1842, as a family home after his marriage. He chose it because it was in the country but close to London and had what he called a "capital [excellent] study" on the ground floor.

journals and notes, which he called his *Journal of Researches into the Natural History and Geology of the Countries Visited During the Voyage of H.M.S. Beagle*. Today, this book is usually known as *The Voyage of the Beagle*. It became very popular and helped Darwin gain even more friends in the world of science.

Slow progress

Darwin's writing work did not always proceed as fast as it might have done, mainly because of family pressures. In January 1839, Darwin married his cousin, Emma Wedgwood. They had a happy marriage and had ten children. Darwin was a very devoted and attentive father. This slowed down his work, as did the fact that he was often unwell.

Breakthrough

Darwin saw the relationships between different species as a "tree of life." It could be shown as a tree-like pattern, with new species splitting off from earlier species to form the branches and twigs—a view accepted to this day.

Evidence for evolution

Bringing the facts together

Following the publication of *The Voyage of the Beagle*, Darwin collected more evidence and made more notes. His task was difficult, because he had so many different discoveries and facts to bring together. Many of them arose from his voyage on the *Beagle*.

Ideas

• Some living things, such as bees and flowers, depend on each other to survive.

Darwin wondered how this had come about. Had they changed to suit each other?

• Darwin looked at the fossil evidence of animals similar to today's creatures, that seemed to have changed.

• He considered the puzzle of the Galapagos finches—so alike, yet different. Had they begun as one species and separated into many? If so, how? And why?

Flowers attract bees, which collect nectar from them, using their long tongues. They also collect pollen on their legs. The bees carry pollen from flower to flower, pollinating the plants, so they can produce seeds. Darwin wondered how it could be that two living things could develop to depend on each other in this way.

- Very different creatures all had similar bodies. For example, humans, birds, bats, and lizards all had a backbone, ribs, four limbs, two eyes, and so on. Had they all developed from one original type of animal?

Nature selects

Darwin was especially interested in selective breeding and how breeders selected the qualities they wanted in their animals. Was something like this happening in nature?

Darwin exchanged letters with many selective breeders. One was William Bernhard Tegetmeier, a leading authority on poultry. In an 1856 letter, Darwin asked for samples of different breeds: "I should be glad of anything . . , which you consider a distinct breed. I should be willing to go to 5^s [5 shillings—half a dollar, or 25 p today] per bird."

Human struggles

Darwin was also influenced by the work of a British philosopher, Thomas Robert Malthus. His most famous work was *An Essay on the Principle of Population*, which he published first in 1798. In it, he said that when the human population increased, people had to struggle for food and work. The weakest and poorest often died young or were swept away by famines and disease.

Darwin saw that this could apply to all living things. Animals often had too many

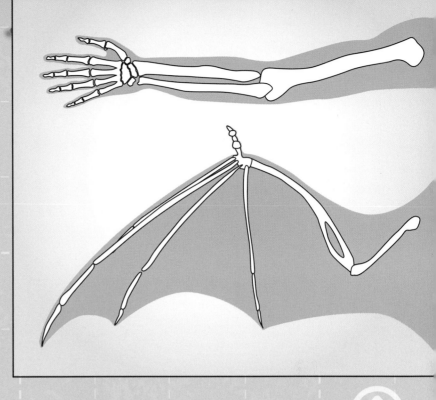

A bat's wing contains similar bones to those found in other animals. Here you can see how like the bones in a human arm they are. The "fingers" are spread out to hold the skin of the wing.

young and most plants made too many seeds for them all to survive. What was special about the survivors? They must be selected—by nature.

"I saw, on reading Malthus on Population, that natural selection was the inevitable result of the rapid increase of all organic beings."
Charles Darwin, in his 1868 book *The Variation of Animals and Plants under Domestication*.

Breakthrough

Studying the work of experts, such as Tegetmeier, and philosophers, such as Malthus, helped Darwin forge ahead with his theory of natural selection.

Darwin's big idea

Finalizing the idea

Through the 1840s and 1850s, Darwin perfected and polished his ideas. He developed an explanation for evolution that he called "natural selection." It works in the way its name suggests—by nature selecting some living things to survive and thrive, and not others.

"From so simple a beginning endless forms most beautiful and most wonderful have been, and are being, evolved."

Charles Darwin, from his book *On the Origin of Species*, 1859.

How it works

• In nature, there are often too many living things to survive, so they have to compete for food and living space. They must also be able to protect themselves from predators and other threats.

• Within each species, slight differences sometimes appear in individuals. Darwin called these "variations." (Today, they are called "**mutations**.") For example, some individuals will be bigger or have different coloring, better eyesight, a slightly longer neck, and so on.

• Depending on factors such as where the species lives, what food it eats, and what predators hunt it, these variations may give some individuals an advantage. These individuals are likely to survive for longer.

• Those that survive longer are likely to have more young and may pass on their

A spider monkey in Costa Rica. Like many other monkeys in South America, it has evolved so that it can use its tail as an extra limb to help it swing among the trees.

"Survival of the fittest"

You may hear the phrase "survival of the fittest" in descriptions of natural selection and evolution. "Fittest" does not mean the healthiest, fastest, or strongest. It just means the most fit, or most suitable. The creatures that "fit" their surroundings best are the ones that survive longest.

These vine snakes have evolved to look like the plants they live among. This helps them survive, as they can hunt for birds to eat without being seen.

features to their young. So the most useful "variations" get "selected" and continue, while less useful ones die out.

• All this means that, in each generation, a particular group of survivors are naturally selected. Over time, this can make the whole species change. The effect will be more marked if the **environment** changes in some way—for example, if there is a change in the climate of a region. This

would make a change in a living thing all the more important for its survival.

• If two groups of the same species live in different places, they could change differently in order to survive in their environments. Eventually, two new species would evolve from one.

Breakthrough

The theory of natural selection was a huge step in the history of science. It showed how species could—and in fact had to—change and diversify over time to suit their surroundings. It also showed that this happened without any deliberate plan or design—just by natural processes.

Out in the open

Making up his mind

Darwin became increasingly sure of his theory of natural selection. Yet he still put off making his ideas public—until something happened to force him to act. In 1856, through his friend Charles Lyell, Darwin heard that another British naturalist, Alfred Russel Wallace, was developing similar ideas to his.

The race to publish

Darwin had planned to write and publish a book on his theory but, in 1858, Wallace wrote to him from southeast Asia, where he was collecting specimens of wildlife. He outlined a theory very similar to natural selection. Darwin realized there was no time to complete a long book. He had to hurry to make his own ideas public, or it would look as if he had copied Wallace.

While in southeast Asia, Wallace discovered flying frogs living in the forests. The frogs have evolved large, webbed feet and flaps of skin along their sides, which they spread out in order to glide from tree to tree.

Alfred Russel Wallace

Date of birth: January 8, 1823

Place of birth: Llanbadoc, Wales

Greatest achievement: Besides developing a theory of natural selection similar to Darwin's (though not as complete), Wallace was a great explorer and naturalist.

Interesting fact: Dozens of living things are named after Wallace, such as Wallace's jewel beetle, Wallace's stripe-faced fruit bat, and Wallace's flying frog.

Date of death: November 7, 1913

At the time, Darwin was very distracted, because his baby son was seriously unwell. Eventually, Lyell and another friend, Joseph Dalton Hooker, arranged for Darwin's and Wallace's ideas to be launched together. They sent a joint paper, made up of both men's work, to the Linnean Society of London. This was—and still is—an important scientific society, whose stated aims are "the cultivation of the Science of Natural History." The paper was first read to a gathering of the society on July 1, 1858, and published the following month.

The reaction

Considering how controversial the theory of natural selection would become, it did not make much of an impact in 1858. This is partly because it did not reach a wide audience at first; it was read by only a

Darwin's study at Down House, as it looked when he worked there. This was where he wrote his books and carried out his research.

small group of scientists. While some agreed with it and some did not, no one was particularly upset or angered by it.

"The year which has passed has not, indeed, been marked by any . . . striking discoveries."

Thomas Bell, the president of the Linnean Society of London, remarking in May 1859 on the previous year's work. Natural selection's great importance had not yet been recognized.

Breakthrough

The new idea of natural selection had entered the public arena—although it was not to become well-known until a little later.

Completing the book

Over the next year, Darwin finally completed a full-length book, explaining his theory of natural selection in detail. It was published in 1859 and entitled *On the Origin of Species by Means of Natural Selection, or the Preservation of Favoured Races in the Struggle for Life*. It is usually known simply as *On the Origin of Species*.

THAT'S A FACT!

Just over a thousand copies of *On the Origin of Species* were printed on November 24, 1859, and the book sold out almost immediately.

Bestseller

Thanks to Darwin's fame as a naturalist and his scientist friends, the book was an instant hit—despite the lack of reaction to the theory a year earlier. Although he had never trained in biology or zoology, Darwin was now at the center of British scientific life. His work was discussed in universities and

A cartoon showing Charles Darwin in the "Evolutionary Tree"—an idea he explained in *On the Origin of Species*. This cartoon, and others like it, appeared in the popular press. It poked fun at Darwin's theory, but, unlike some later cartoons, it was not particularly unkind.

Thomas Huxley

Date of birth: May 4, 1825

Place of birth: Ealing, England

Greatest achievement: Huxley was a leading expert on animal anatomy. His studies of animal skeletons and fossils revealed how species were related to each other.

Interesting fact: Because he supported Darwin's views and stood in for him in debates, Huxley was nicknamed "Darwin's bulldog."

Date of death: June 29, 1895

museums, in national newspapers, and in thousands of homes.

Darwin himself, however, was unwell and suffering from grief over the deaths of two of his children. Because of this, he did not actively join these debates.

An angry reaction?

Today, many people think *On the Origin of Species* was met with a furious reaction from religious believers, and that Darwin became a figure of hate. In fact, that is far from the truth. Some Christians did get very upset. Robert Fitzroy, Darwin's old captain, was one, and Darwin's own wife, Emma, could not reconcile her religious beliefs with her husband's work. Some saw the book as **heresy** and burned it. A few turned up to scientific meetings and shouted abuse at Darwin's supporters.

But many Christians were actually open to Darwin's ideas. Instead of dismissing natural selection, they thought about how the theory could fit in with religious teachings. There were many calm debates, held in meetings, in the press, and in letters. As Darwin was preoccupied, his friend Thomas Huxley often argued his case for him.

Breakthrough

On the Origin of Species was one of the most important books ever published. It started a new field of evolutionary science.

Darwin's great works

Further writing

On the Origin of Species was just the start. Over the next 22 years, Darwin published several important works, such as *The Expression of Emotions in Man and Animals*, *The Power of Movement in Plants*, and *The Formation of Vegetable Mould Through the Action of Worms*. (Earthworms were one of Darwin's favorite subjects of study.)

Descended from apes

After *On the Origin of Species*, the most famous of Darwin's other books was *The Descent of Man*. Published in 1871, it was a study of the human species, the different races, human features and qualities, and how humans had developed from earlier animals. Darwin argued that humans had evolved from early apes.

A cartoon published in *The Hornet* in 1871 showing Darwin as an ape with the head of a man. Cartoons like this appeared in the popular press and reflected the outrage some people felt at Darwin's theory that humans were descended from apes.

"From what my friends who go into society say, everybody is talking about it without being shocked."

Charles Darwin discussing the reaction to *The Descent of Man*, recalled in 1884 by his friend, J. D. Hague.

Another kind of natural selection

In *The Descent of Man*, Darwin described another kind of natural selection that was not just about "survival of the fittest." It is called sexual selection. Most animals do not **reproduce** just because they have survived, but because they have selected the best individual they can find as a mate. So some animals, such as the peacock, with its beautiful tail, have evolved striking displays to help them attract a mate. Though such a display might not help the individual survive, it may indicate healthiness. It will impress the opposite sex, so increasing the animal's chances of having plenty of offspring.

The peacock's tail is an example of how animals—especially male birds—develop displays to attract mates. The male has far more color than the female, which, by contrast, appears rather drab.

These were related to today's chimpanzees, but they gradually developed human qualities, such as complex language and culture, and greater intelligence.

However, Darwin said that humans were still animals. The difference between us and other animals was "one of degree and not of kind." In other words, humans are just more advanced animals.

Talk of the town

Again, this idea went against traditional Christian teachings, which said that God had created humans as they are now and in his image. But again, British society was less upset than Darwin expected. Some people did criticize him, and he was mocked in some newspapers. But he was surprised and pleased that most people took his ideas on board and talked about them, instead of just getting angry.

Breakthrough

The idea of the evolution of humans from apes was not completely new, but *The Descent of Man* explained it clearly and made a solid scientific argument for it.

What are genes?

Today, we know a lot about **genes**—the tiny parts inside the cells of living things that control the way those things live, work and grow. It is thanks to genes that qualities such as body shape and strength get passed on from one generation to the next. It is easy to see how important genes can be to survival—and, as a result, are key to natural selection. Darwin did not know this, because when he published *On the Origin of Species*, they had not been discovered.

Reproducing sexually

Most animals and many plants reproduce "sexually." That means they produce special cells for reproduction—male sex cells and female ones. Each male sex cell contains half the genes needed to make a new living thing like its parent. Each female sex cell contains the other half. When the two cells join, a new life begins with all the genes it needs. These are a unique mix of both parents' genes.

Mendel and his peas

However, at the same time as Darwin was writing, a monk in a monastery in what is now the Czech Republic, was taking

Mendel crossed a pea plant with white flowers with one with pink flowers. The resulting flowers were pink. Plants grown from seeds that formed after pollinating these pink flowers with their own pollen were sometimes white. The whiteness was inside the plant, but not always visible.

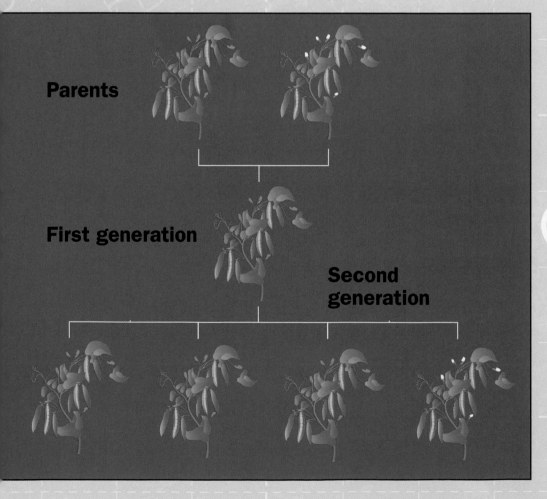

Parents

First generation

Second generation

Gregor Mendel

Date of birth: July 22, 1822

Place of birth: Heinzendorf bei Odrau, in today's Czech Republic

Greatest achievement: Mendel's studies of how pea plants passed on their qualities paved the way for the discovery of genes.

Interesting fact: Although they lived at the same time, Darwin had probably never heard of Mendel or his work.

Date of death: January 6, 1884

"I am convinced that it will not be long before the whole world acknowledges the results of my work."
Gregor Mendel, writing in 1865, in *The Proceedings of Brünn Society for Natural Science.*

the first steps toward discovering and understanding genes. Through the 1850s and 1860s, this monk, Gregor Mendel, studied **heredity** (how qualities are passed on through generations) in pea plants in his monastery garden. He saw how qualities such as pea shape, plant height, and flower color seemed to be "carried" from one generation to the next—although this was not always apparent in every plant.

Mendel decided there were things, which he called "factors," that carried the qualities from one generation to the next. He also realized that, when plants had two parents, they inherited some factors from each—although, sometimes a factor carried might not show up until a later generation.

Later, scientists identified these factors inside cells, and they were renamed genes.

Breakthrough

Gregor Mendel's work was the first real study of genes, though it would not be recognized until after his death.

Understanding genes

What are genes?

During the 20th century, scientists discovered more about genes. They discovered that they are in the cells of the bodies of living things, what they are made of, and how they work. They also found out how they are passed on from parents to their young.

Recipe for a species

Each species has its own set of genes—or **genome**. This controls how cells grow, and so decides things like the creature's size, shape, and color. For example, among animals, a leopard genome contains instructions for making big, strong, spotty, furry hunters. The genome each offspring inherits from its parents is basically the same as for other members of its species, but it will have very slight differences. For example, you and your friend might have different hair and eye color, because you each have a unique mix of gene patterns, inherited from both your parents.

How genes and DNA work

Toward the middle of the 1900s, scientists found that genes were made of strands of a substance called deoxyribonucleic acid, or **DNA**. In 1950, a scientist named

Although all people have almost identical sets of genes, there are very tiny differences. These are what make us all look different, giving us light or dark hair or skin, making us tall or short, and so on.

Chromosomes and genes

In most species, each cell contains strands of DNA, called **chromosomes**. Each chromosome contains many genes. Each gene is a sequence of DNA, containing a pattern of chemicals that cells can "read" as instructions.

This picture shows James Watson (right) and Francis Crick (left) in 1953, after they had worked out the structure of the DNA molecule. Crick and Watson won a Nobel prize for their work in 1962.

Rosalind Franklin took a special type of photograph of a molecule of DNA. This showed it had a double helix (spiral) shape, like a twisted ladder. In 1953, James Watson and Francis Crick worked out how DNA carried instructions to make cells work, using patterns of four different chemicals as a kind of code.

They also found out DNA made copies of itself for new cells by splitting its "ladder" in half and building two new matching strands. As DNA copies itself, changes or mutations sometimes occur within it. Some mutations can be passed on from parents to offspring and introduce variations between individuals.

Some mutations are useful. We saw on page 28 how this affects evolution. For example, a mutation in an animal's DNA might make it better-equipped to survive than others of the same species. It might make it stronger than either of its parents or give it better eyesight or some other useful feature. As a result, very slowly, and over many generations, the species will change.

Breakthrough

Understanding DNA allows scientists to study the way that species' genomes have changed over time and to compare the genomes of different species. This helps them find out more about evolution.

Was Darwin right?

Today's science

Almost all scientists today agree that natural selection happens and that it is an important explanation for the evolution of living things. Darwin's discovery still stands as one of the most significant ever in biology. But his work was not the end of the story. Today, the evolution of living things is a major area of biology.

A highly magnified view of swine flu viruses, which caused a flu epidemic that swept the world in 2009. It was not a particularly dangerous version of flu, but doctors are worried that mutations could turn it into a mass killer.

THAT'S A FACT!

Germs breed so fast that they give scientists a way to study evolution in action. For example, the virus that causes flu, a dangerous disease, evolves so quickly that every year it is slightly different from before. By studying its genes, scientists can now see how this happens. This helps them find ways to fight the disease.

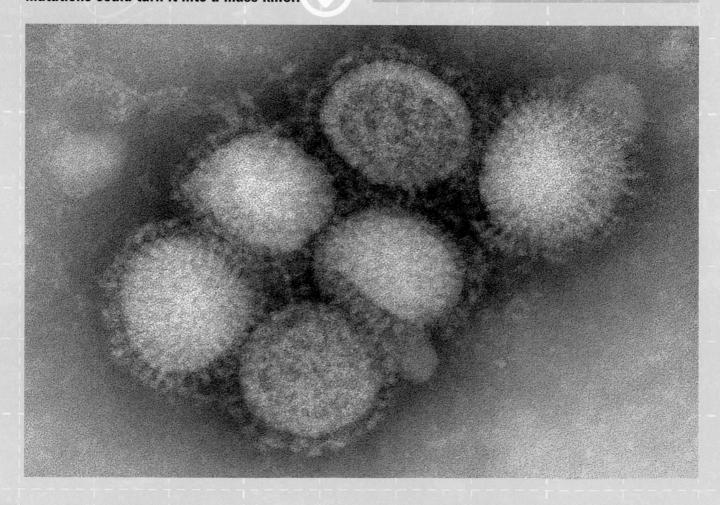

Richard Dawkins

Date of birth: March 26, 1941

Place of birth: Nairobi, Kenya

Greatest achievement: Dawkins has built on the work of previous scientists, and extended ideas about what evolution means and what it can affect.

Interesting fact: In modern debates about natural selection and evolution, Dawkins has been attacked far more for opposing traditional religious views than Darwin himself ever was.

Date of death: Still living

New discoveries

When a scientist comes up with a new idea, it rarely gives all the answers. Darwin's theory was no exception. But he had made a breakthrough that paved the way for more discoveries and debates. Biologists continue to study evolution and have come up with new ideas about it ever since. New methods and equipment have allowed them to study things like how viruses (tiny germs) evolve and how genes can switch themselves on and off over time.

Memes

Dawkins also described **memes**, which are like genes, but are actually aspects of culture, like a hairstyle or a catchphrase. They survive or die out, are copied and passed on, and evolve, in a similar way to biological genes.

New ideas

Meanwhile, others came up with theories that refined and improved on Darwin's ideas. For example, in 1976, British biologist Richard Dawkins, in his book *The Selfish Gene*, argued that natural selection selects genes, rather than creatures, to be reproduced, and that genes use animals and plants as vehicles to help them survive. Other scientists have found ways of moving genes between different kinds of unrelated living things, changing them in ways that natural selection alone cannot.

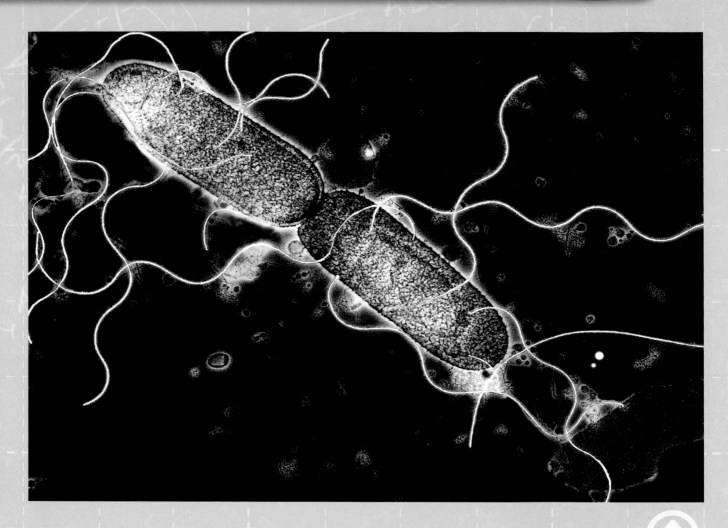

Natural selection continues

Natural selection is not just something that happened in the past—it is still going on. Living things are becoming extinct and species are changing and separating into new species. Changing environments and climate constantly force species to adapt to suit their new surroundings. There is still plenty for evolutionary scientists to find out.

Are humans still evolving?

Some people have suggested that humans have stopped evolving, as most humans

This picture shows bacteria in the human intestines as they reproduce by dividing into two almost identical parts. They are continuing to evolve today—for example, bacteria can develop resistance to antibiotic medicine.

can now survive to adulthood and reproduce thanks to modern medicine. But in fact, humans are still evolving. There are always new mutations in our genes that make our genome change over time. New diseases come along that kill some people, while others are better suited to surviving that disease, and so are "selected" by nature.

No one knows if, or how, humans will change their appearance or shape in the future. But several writers and artists have speculated about how humans or other living things could evolve over the thousands and millions of years to come.

Antibiotic resistance

One example of ongoing evolution is **antibiotic** resistance. When we try to kill harmful bacteria with antibiotics, some bacteria may survive. They are the "fittest"—those best suited to surviving the medicine and being selected by nature. If they are able to breed, they pass on their qualities, such as antibiotic resistance, to the next generation.

Over time, this leads to new, more deadly, strains of bacteria that are harder for us to treat. This is one reason why your doctor tells you to take all the antibiotics you are given—to make sure you wipe out as many germs as possible and don't give them a chance to breed.

Helping each other

One thing evolutionary scientists are still arguing about is why some animals, including humans, look after each other. If all individuals were simply struggling to survive, we would surely just compete with each other. Some scientists think that genes encourage us to care for members of our species so that the whole species' genes get passed on. Some think that evolving caring genes helps us survive, as if we care for others, they will want to care for us. We see this especially clearly in the way that, in most societies, people go out of their way to help relatives, who share even more of their genes than other people.

Meerkats are small mammals related to mongooses. They have evolved to live in groups in the deserts of southern Africa and are well-known for the way all the members of the group take care of one another.

Glossary

antibiotic a medicine that kills bacteria

bacteria tiny, single-celled organisms. Some kinds carry disease.

biology the study of living things

chart to make a map of something, especially a coastline or area of sea

chromosomes strands of DNA found inside cells, along which genes are found

divine holy or to do with a god or gods

DNA (deoxyribonucleic acid) the substance that genes are made of

environment another word for surroundings

evolution the way species of living things change over time from one generation to the next

extinct an extinct species is one that has died out completely and no longer exists

femur the large bone in the thigh of humans and many other animals

folklore the myths and fairy stories of a culture

fossil remains of a living thing preserved as a shape or mark in stone

genes units of information, found inside cells, that control the way a living thing grows, lives, and functions

genome the complete set of genes belonging to a particular species or living thing

geologist someone who studies geology —the science of earth and its rocks

habitat the surroundings in which a species lives, such as a forest, seashore, or desert

heredity the way the qualities and features of living things are passed on from one generation to the next in their genes

heresy a challenge to, or an attack on, an established religious belief

landform a feature of the land, such as a mountain, beach, or cliff

magnitude size

meme an idea, fashion, or phrase that is passed on from generation to generation and that, like a gene, may gradually change as this happens

mutation a change that occurs when DNA copies itself, which can result in a change or new feature appearing in a species

natural selection the way in which some individual creatures are more likely to survive and have young, depending on how well-suited they are to their natural surroundings

naturalist someone who studies the natural world

plankton a mass of small living things that float near the surface of the sea

predator a living thing that hunts, kills, and eats animals

prehistoric from the time before history began to be written down

reproduce to have young

selective breeding selecting particular farm animals, pets, or crops to breed from, in order to control the way a species develops

species a particular type of living thing. A living thing can usually only reproduce with other members of its own species

strata a name for the different layers found in rock

survey ship a ship dedicated to charting, mapping, and taking measurements as it makes its journey

taxidermist someone who practices taxidermy—preserving dead animals to be displayed

theory an explanation for something that happens, based on the evidence available

uniformitarianism a theory developed by James Hutton that says the earth's rocks and landforms have formed, worn away, and reformed many times

variation a name for the slight differences between living things that belong to the same species

Further information

Books

Charles and Emma: The Darwins Leap of Faith by Deborah Heiligman. Henry Holt and Co., 2008.

Evolution Revolution by Robert Winston. Dorling Kindersley, 2009.

Genetics by Anna Claybourne. Chelsea House, 2006.

Genetics: From DNA to Designer Dogs by Kathleen Simpson. National Geographic Society, 2008.

Inside the Beagle with Charles Darwin by Fiona Macdonald. Book House, 2005.

On the Origin of Species by Charles Darwin. Penguin Group, 2003. (One of many editions.)

Some useful websites

NOVA's Evolution Project
www.pbs.org/wgbh/evolution
Website developed in conjunction with the TV series; includes videos, a resource library, activities, and more.

The Complete Work of Charles Darwin Online
darwin-online.org.uk
Access to the full texts of Darwin's books, diaries, and papers.

Tree of Life
www.wellcometreeoflife.org
Interactive website that lets you find out how living things are related to each other, with pictures, videos, and facts.

science.howstuffworks.com/evolution/natural-selection.htm
Find out about natural selection and evolution and look at some specific case studies showing natural selection in action.

Index